Families

Grandparents

Rebecca Rissman

www.raintreepublishers.co.uk

Visit our website to find out more information about Raintree books.

To order:

☎ Phone 0845 6044371

▤ Fax +44 (0) 1865 312263

✉ Email myorders@raintreepublishers.co.uk

Customers from outside the UK please telephone +44 1865 312262

Raintree is an imprint of Capstone Global Library Limited, a company incorporated in England and Wales having its registered office at 7 Pilgrim Street, London, EC4V 6LB – Registered company number: 6695582

Text © Capstone Global Library Limited 2011
First published in hardback in 2011
The moral rights of the proprietor have been asserted.

Edited by Rebecca Rissman, Dan Nunn, and Catherine Veitch
Designed by Ryan Frieson
Picture research by Tracy Cummins
Production by Victoria Fitzgerald
Originated by Capstone Global Library
Printed and bound in China by Leo Paper Products Ltd

ISBN 978 1 406 22148 0
14 13 12 11 10
10 9 8 7 6 5 4 3 2 1

British Library Cataloguing in Publication Data
Rissman, Rebecca.
Grandparents. -- (Families)
306.8'745-dc22

Acknowledgements

We would like to thank the following for permission to reproduce photographs: Corbis pp.**10** (©Markus Moellenberg), **14** (©Kevin Dodge), **19** (©Nils Hendrik Muller/Cultura), **20** (©Kristy-Anne Glubish/Design Pics), **23 c** (©Markus Moellenberg); Getty Images pp. **4** (Sylvain Grandadam), **7** (Stephen Chiang), **8** (Tony Metaxas), **9** (Jupiterimages), **11** (Jay Reilly), **13** (Manoj Adlukay), **16** (Ron Levine), **17** (Image Source), **18** (Alex Mares-Manton), **21** (Ariel Skelley), **23 a** (Manoj Adlukay); istockphoto pp. **5** (©Ann Marie Kurtz), **22** (©Diane Labombarbe); Photolibrary pp. **12** and **23 b** (both Radius Images); Shutterstock pp. **6** (©Mehmet Dilsiz), **15** (©Yarek Gora).
Front cover photograph of a granddaughter kissing her grandmother reproduced with permission of Getty Images (China Tourism Press). Back cover photograph of a granddaughter helping her grandfather with his tie reproduced with permission of Corbis (©Nils Hendrik Muller/Cultura).

We would like to thank Anne Pezalla, Dee Reid and Diana Bentley for their invaluable help in the preparation of this book.

Every effort has been made to contact copyright holders of material reproduced in this book. Any omissions will be rectified in subsequent printings if notice is given to the publisher.

Contents

What is a family? 4

What are families like? 8

Who are grandparents? 10

Different grandparents 12

Family tree 22

Picture glossary 23

Index 24

What is a family?

A family is a group of people who care for each other.

Leabharlanna Poibli Chathair Bhaile Átha Cliath
Dublin City Public Libraries

People in a family are different ages.

All families are different.

All families are special.

What are families like?

Some families like to play games.

Some families like to cook together.

Who are grandparents?

In a family there are parents. Parents are adults who have children.

grandparent

Parents have parents, too!
They are called grandparents.

Different grandparents

Your parent's mother is
your grandmother.

Your parent's father is
your grandfather.

Some families have
many grandparents.

Some families have few grandparents.
Some families do not have any
grandparents.

Some grandparents live far from their families.

Some grandparents live with
their families.

Some grandparents care for their grandchildren.

Some grandchildren help care for
their grandparents.

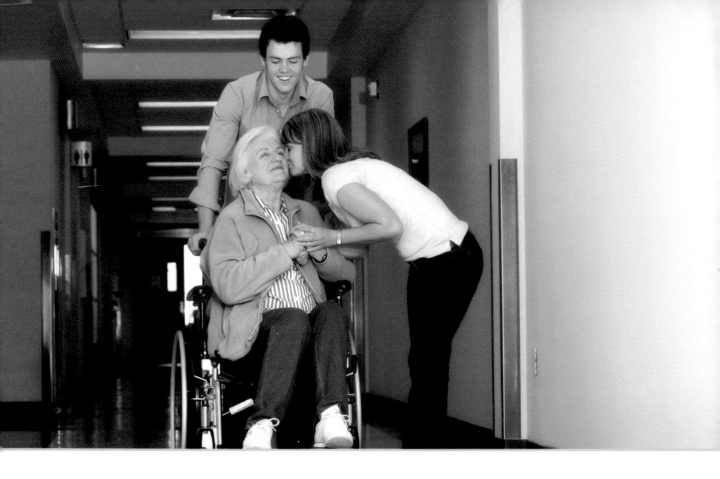

Some families visit their grandparents at special homes.

Do you have grandparents?

Family tree

Grandmother | Grandfather | Grandmother | Grandfather

Mother | Father

You

Picture glossary

 **grandfather** a parent's father

 **grandmother** a parent's mother

 **parent** adult who has children

Index

grandfather 13, 22

grandmother 12, 22

grandparents 11, 14, 15, 16, 17, 18, 19, 20, 21, 22

parent 10, 11, 12, 13, 22

Note to parents and teachers
Before reading
Explain to children that people in families are often related to each other. Most children are related to their parents. And parents have parents, too! They are a child's grandparents!

After reading
Ask children if they have special nicknames for their grandparents, such as Granny or Grandpa. Make a list of these names on the board.